cover photo: "Big Easy, Volume 2 for 2", design Ron Arad 1988.
cover lay out: Patrick Lebédeff

editor assistant: Stéphane Argillet

Special Thanks to:

Alban Barré, Elisabeth Lagane, Yannick Haennel, Caroline Thorman, Gilbert Aurejac, Cathy Lenihan.

© ÉDITIONS DIS VOIR
3, RUE BEAUTREILLIS
75004 PARIS

ISBN 2-906-571-59-8

PRINTED IN EUROPE

RON ARAD

Ouvrage aidé par le
Ministère français chargé de la Culture

this series edited by
PIERRE STAUDENMEYER

in the same series

ANDREA BRANZI
François Burkhardt, Cristina Morozzi

RON ARAD

RAYMOND GUIDOT

OLIVIER BOISSIÈRE

CONTENTS

From Jerusalem to London:
the Early Days of a Creative Imagination

*I*n London, where he has been working since 1981, Ron Arad is very much a creator from another world. Originally that world was Israel, where he studied at the Jerusalem Academy of Art from 1971-1973, before coming to Great Britain to complete his architectural training and play his part in the great anti-authoritarian movement then sweeping the western world.

Having been a force for freedom in the 1960s, by the following decade the storm had gathered a more destructive force. This change can be seen in the constantly-changing provocations of the fashion scene, from the Mary Quant mini-skirt, through the weird carnaval gaiety of hippy fancy dress, to the slashed and tattered rags of late 70s punk.

It was in this period that London became Ron Arad's home base. At the prestigious Architectual Association School his teachers were Bernard Tschumi and Peter Cook, the promotor of an architectural utopia, a polyvalent dream launched in 1963 by the creation of the Archigram Group, which he co-founded. This encounter between Arad and Cook, in a place which would later be largely ruled by the principles of "architectural deconstructivism", proved fruitful. Although Ron Arad escapes simple classification, it is not hard to imagine the spirit of Archigram behind his 1981 "Transformer" seat, a bag full of polystyrene beads out which the air was sucked by an ordinary domestic vacuum cleaner so that it hardened comfortably in the shape of the sitter. The same is true of the "Aerial Light" rotating telescopic lamp of 1982, which could be moved by remote control. It is scarcely surprising that objects of this kind are also found in projects by Peter Cook such as "Informaison" of 1968, or his 1969 "Instant City". But this line of development, with its logical extension in the direction of high technology, is not really the most central aspect of Arad's creative thinking.

A Subversive Experimenter

He quickly developed a preference for a different approach, the craftsman-like mastery of more "solid" materials. Materials which, for the most part, had long since proved their worth, but on which he made even greater demands in his own very unusual experimental environment.

Peter Cook admired the rapid development of his uncommonly talented former student who, after graduating from the Architectural Association in 1979, had by 1981 already founded (with Caroline Thorman) the "One-Off" London show-room and studio located in Covent Garden. In July 1988 he wrote in the

Box In 4 Movements, 1994.
A cube in 4 sections connected to each other via ratchet hinges. The cube can disintegrate to any shape of a chair or small table and freeze in any position.

catalogue of a Ron Arad exhibition at the Vitra Design Museum in Weil am Rhein: "The most characteristic thing about Ron Arad is that he fights on two fronts. On the one hand he adds red robot blood to a basic halogen lamp, so that we can change its expression using a remote control. Three years later he installs a complete hi-fi system in a kind of concrete castle." – a reference to the now-famous "Concrete Stereo", whose components (record deck, tuner, speakers) are moulded into rough-cast concrete blocks full of gaps and cracks which reveal an underlying crude steel framework suggestive of decay: something like a demolition site in miniature.

A creation like this immediately made Ron Arad into the leader of a subversive school of design quite close in spirit to the "destroy" attitude cultivated by punks. Along the way he ran into Nigel Coates, another A.A. "old boy" (he left as Ron arrived) who, as a member of the "Nato" group which designed shop interiors to look as if they had been bombed or subjected to an armed robbery, was championing a "culture of the street". What the reproducible "Concrete Stereo" confirmed above all, an objective also dear to Gaetano Pesce, was that differentiation could be introduced into a serial production process. Though similar from one to the next, each object is made subtly different by the controlled introduction of manufacturing flaws. In fact, for Ron as for Gaetano, it was the material left to its own devices that called the tune, through its unwillingness to accommodate itself to the mould. It was not long before his attention shifted towards the material's "skin" as it contorted under the impact of pressure or the action of fire.

An Encounter with Equipment of Torture and Liberation

As Jean Prouvé had done sixty years earlier, Ron Arad discovered in the mid 80s the virtues of sheet steel. As it emerges, thin and flexible, from the rolling mill, it possesses no real mechanical strength. But once bent or folded it stiffens and becomes able to resist efforts to compress, flex or twist it. If two edges are brought together and welded, a hollow shape can be formed of comparable strength to a much heavier solid of identical volume. His first constructions in bent and welded sheet steel were made up of cones and cylinders arranged on top of each other. Some were masterpieces, including "Shadow of Time", the combined lamp and clock of 1986 which projected the time on the ceiling.

Already the decisive battle between Arad and what was to become his favourite material was underway. He worked with his bare hands, refusing the limitations and anaemic perfection to which the use of machines would lead. Imperfect curvatures show the marks of tools, but above all of sheer muscular effort. In the heat of the welding torch the metal also started to twist and take on new colours, turning redder or bluer at the points where it melted (it is worth pointing out that for Arad it is almost always the material that gives the object its colour). The struggle continued. When the partitioned forms made their appearance, their corner weldings twisted the sheet metal until it curled up, flared out or became pitted.

Then, in a world now bristling with tortured forms, organic models began to come back into their own, and the "Tinker Chair"

Box In 4 Movements, 1994.

of 1988 looks like pieces of sawn-up bone (hip-bone, perhaps). Sculpture thus won out in the end, so that even if Arad's steel cut-outs started off identical, the way they were assembled introduced a generalised dissimilarity. The whole of habitable space now started to obey the same law, with even partitions and walls being made of steel formed and coloured by the torch-flame. These were separating and dividing walls, walls that concealed.

Games with Opaqueness and Transparency

This absence of transparency and visual penetrability doubt-less posed the kind of challenge that Ron enjoys, for he always knows in advance that he will find some sort of answer: his sort.

Now that the one-off piece had converged with the earlier experimental ones, Arad took the opportunity to linger over his researches into materials and the subtleties of their use. Particular-ly those that allowed him to use effects ranging from complete opaqueness to transparency, with all the tricks and illusions of translucidity in between. Steel could easily be perforated until it looked like lace, allowing him to play around with bits of a hidden image seen through the holes in an opaque, superimposed silhouette. A simple way indeed of adapting the traditional idea of a cut-out screen to the requirements of a personal aesthetic.

Roughening the edges of a sheet of glass, engraving it and then blasting it with sand, is also a traditional procedure that has the advantage of introducing a play of vague shadows half-seen beneath the network of closely-hatched lines or behind the frosted surface.

That is how Arad created his mysterious table tops. For all that, the basic material and the ways of working with it were still those of the traditonal craftsman, and he wanted to go much further, both in the incongruity of the initial choice of materials and in the ways they were subjected to the whims of his demanding creativity.

Thus the next material to be tried out was "honey-comb" alluminium of the kind developed for making very light aircraft floors. Looked at straight on, it appears transparent, but from an oblique angle it goes back to being opaque. In between, it lends itself to all kinds of subtle concealments. Arad used it to make astonishing lamp-shades, like monstrous insect-wings, for unlikely-looking standard-lamps, or as the ideal material for room screens of ever-changing degrees of discretion, strangely haunted by shadows of giants or barking dogs (a rare concession to figuration). As these "Deep Screens" evolved into sections of partition, proper room-dividers, he fitted them with casters to give them a more obvious mobility, a long way from the inconvenience of the basic folding screen.

Playful Ambiguities

We are now in 1987 and the universe gradually created by Ron Arad has become all the stranger because, while continuing to fulfill their original functions, the objects which compose it have been enriched with new values, extensions of old utilitarian ones, but strongly shifted in a playful direction. Being able to control a movable lamp from a distance certainly increases its usefulness, but

Pic-Chairs, 1997.
A small series of 20 handmade and unique chairs. In fibre-glass + polyester with pure
pigments, tissues, ground metals & lights.
ph: Wilhelm Moser

it also means you can play with it like a remote-control toy plane or car. Being able to read the time on the bedroom ceiling, with the added benefit of indirect lighting, allows you to reconnect with your living space the moment you wake up, as you lie in bed. But, thanks to the shadow with its mysterious messages moving around above your head, it also lets your dreams merge into disconcerting day-dreams. Semi-transparent mobile panels allow you to divide space without really partitioning it. But, to quote Peter Cook, they also mean you can "play with the ambiguity between what is seen and what is only glimpsed" – a kind of hide-and-seek game.

And while it is true that when, in the salvage tradition of Achille and Pier Giacomo Castiglioni, Arad fitted a Rover 2000 seat to a tubular structure to make a reclining arm-chair, he was behaving like an ergonomist whose only concern is with function, in the design of the "Tinker Chair" or the "Italian Fish", symbolic, ludic and artistic values come back to the fore. Gaetano Pesce, in suggesting that his own creations tend to combine usefulness with something rather more ineffable, speaks of the object as having a "double meaning". This phrase perfectly fits the objects designed by Arad. As a remarkable craftsman able to give form to his own fantasies, he is the first to be astonished by the incongruity that expresses itself through him; as a sculptor, he admires the way the shape develops; as a magician, he is instantly taken in by the success of his tricks.

From Unclassifiable Individual to International Phenomenon

But in the last few years, attentive observers have been surprised by the changing methods of this extraordinary creator whose works invite more than just contemplation. "Please touch", "Please sit here", they seem to say to anyone looking at them. Which is enough to differentiate them from the creations of "artists", who live in fear – a fear shared more intensely still by their buyers (collectors or museum curators) – that fleshly contact will damage the object's precious "skin".

Those observers attentive to the evolution of an *œuvre* with such unexpected shifts of direction are enthusiasts, art critics, museum people, organisers of international events, and publishers. Ron Arad's international reputation blossomed quickly. In 1987 he had exhibitions at several galleries, including "One Off Paris" at the Galerie Yves Gastou (Paris) and "Subject Matter" at the Edward Tatah Gallery (London). He also took part in international forums such as the Kassel "Documenta", and in the same year was one of the designers chosen to represent "New Developments in Design" at the Pompidou Centre as part of its tenth birthday celebrations. Deyan Sudjic points to the subversive character of his presentation, which he describes as follows: "He installed a hydraulic crusher in the gallery and invited exhibition-goers to feed chairs to the monster and watch them being turned in a few seconds into regular cubes of metal, which he then used to build a wall across the gallery." In an article in *Le Jardin des Modes* in October 1992, Christine Colin observes: "Thus Ron Arad set out, with the help of this enormous machine, to boost the consumer cycle's 'turnover'". Ron Arad himself claims to have been performing "a sacrifice to change and the future, to separation and the final parting". This iconoclastic act was no doubt an expression of the urge felt by any young creator to ditch the heavy burden of the past with all speed, but in Arad's case

The "bridge" leading to mezzanine office, steel partition wall of mezzanine office and conference room.
Design: Ron Arad and Alison Brooks.
Ph: Christoph Kicherer.

it also shows a noteworthy ability to free himself from frames of reference which, instinctively, he does not regard as serious anchor-points. He operates with particular freedom with respect to the cultural movements which have come and gone in the western world since the end of the last century: he is able to refer to them all and sweep them aside when he has finished, but also to circumvent or twist them to his own ends. This explains the development of his furniture and architectural work in a direction which cannot be tied down, either, to those "post-modern" trends which, in recent decades, have enshrined the researches of certain other creators in a mythical anteriority.

Dance within Boundless Bounds

Beginning by hijacking an industrial product (in this case the "Kee Klamp" scaffolding system) in the service of the everyday environment – this in a comparable spirit to the tendency that grew up in the New York lofts taken over by artists, and strangely christened "High Tech" by Susan Slesin and Joan Kron –, Arad from the start combined references to the Modern Movement of the 1930s with a working method akin to that of the "radical" designers of the 70s. But his explorations took on their real meaning, and arguably attained a style of their own, in relation to the punk "destroy" movement of the 80s, of which he became one of the main representatives. Then it was time to change tack, since for Arad, if there is one path to follow at all costs, it is the continual deepening of his knowledge of the demands that can be placed on a material when pushing it to its limits. Now, confident of its remarkable capabilities, he began doing battle, hard and crucial, with steel, which gave rise to works born out of an encounter between brutal action and spontaneous reaction. The sheet metal responded to his workman-like attacks with deformations which obeyed certain laws of probability. Such physical effects of chance can be read in the reflections of the worked metal after polishing, particularly in the case of stainless steel. This flexibility of material and form, and mastery of reflections, were qualities brought into his *œuvre* by the creation in 1986 of the "Well Tempered Chair". They mark a change of direction which would soon become fundamental.

"Well Tempered Chair", a re-working, after Philppe Stark's "Richard III", of the archetypal image of the club armchair, relies on the elastic strength of a set of stainless steel leaves tensioned by bending and simply bolted together, without welding. The result is a play of surfaces with self-expressed curves which, although minimalist in spirit, also gesture towards the fluid line dear to both Art Nouveau and Baroque. A new mode of creation was thus founded, one which excluded almost nothing on principle, but was the expression of a formal universe based on a new complicity between a creator and his materials.

The forms which now came into being were the fruits of freely accepted constraints or, more accurately, the result of a mutual non-aggression pact. The metal reacted with simplicity to the simple boiler-making techniques applied to it. While it sometimes curved to make the line and surfaces it was asked to describe more

Two *Schizzo Chairs*, 1994 (Ply by Vitra International) in a tight fit aluminium box.
The box is a chair in its own right. So each "box" makes 3 chairs.
Design: Ron Arad.

fluid, at others it would remain perfectly flat despite the welding, which at the end of the 80s was perhaps not exactly the desired effect.

Controlled Imperfection in the Service of Differentiation... and Perfection as the Ultimate Challenge

The various versions of the "Big Easy" armchair of 1989 demonstrate the degree of control that Arad can exert over a form which is repeated overall from one object to the next, while incorporating desired, even deliberate, surface "defects" which are not the result of technical difficulties. Spoiling the geometrical perfection of the theoretical volume, these defects introduce subtle differences between objects of the same (albeit craftsman-made) series, preserving them, like those of Gaetano Pesce, from un-seemly repetition.

Only a few months later such defects were to be outlawed, as formal perfection became the new golden rule. This shift towards "faultless" results was very much related to new effects Arad found he could obtain by different ways of treating the steel surface, ranging from the matt, colourful appearance of the raw sheet-metal to the polished brilliance of the finished product, reflective as a distorting mirror. Thus varied surface states could enhance the appearance of the same object. The top of "Three Legs and a Table" (1989) retained the matt coloured surface of the raw metal, while the fat cylindrical legs were polished to a faultless finish, as proved by their reflections. As for the "Little Heavy" chair of the same year, highly polished all over, the concave surfaces of the seat and back contained intentional distortions which broke up the reflected image. For this intentionally crude panel-beating operation, Arad used a hard rubber mallet which would not damage the metal. Whether or not they are polished can differentiate two objects of identical shape, a possibility that he exploited in, for instance, "Rolling Volume", a tilting armchair of 1990.

Trapped Reflections and Anamorphic Games

This sophisticated play with the work's surface became as important for Arad as it was for Brancusi, but also, in the 1930s, for the American "Streamline" designers. When a surface is polished to perfection, the quality of the reflection reveals the accuracy of its form. But does this not also relate back to Arad's interest in the incongruous possibilities of honeycomb aluminium? A screen made of this material plays games with the whole of its immediate environment, which it conceals or reveals to a greater or lesser degree depending on the viewing angle. In a comparable if not identical way, the everyday environment was captured and reflected in the distorting mirrors of Arad's polished surfaces. Once again, however, as if to demonstrate his mastery of his resources he would twist the effect achieved: whereas reflected objects are normally external to the mirror, he had the idea of trapping them inside it. "Chair by its Cover" (1989-90) took a perfectly ordinary mass-produced wooden chair and transformed it, by means of its anamorphic image reflected in a concave mirror

London Papardelle, 1992
Flexible low chair profiles in black steel welded onto a section of a woven polished
stainless steel "rug". The "rug" can be rolled, the reel forming a footrest.
design Ron Arad
ph: Christoph Kicherer

which literally surrounds the chair, into a strangely surrealistic object.

A Language of Forms Rooted in Ancient Hebrew Writing

The early 90s were characterised in design by the adoption of a pure, flexible and at times sinuous line (Victor Horta's work, for instance, has been described as having a "whip-like" line). Now that pressed shapes were no longer in favour, designers were making highly systematic use of cylindrical surfaces, in a wider sense of the term than its dictionary definition (the generatrix moving around a circle): a surface generated by a line moving in parallel to a fixed direction along a curved plane (directrix). A particular characteristic of the cylindrical forms designed by Ron Arad is that to date, the generatrix has always been perpendicular to the plane of the directrix, which gives the whole object the appearance of a slice through a profile of constant cross-section.

As they developed towards more undulating forms, his furniture pieces (one might think of the "After Spring" chaise longue, the "Looploop" chairs or "London Papardelle" of 1992) certainly re-discovered a fluidity of line reminiscent of the Baroque or Art Nouveau. However, both the line's flexibility and the meaning of the form it generates refer equally clearly to the cursive writing of the Hebrew alphabet.

Thus, the silhouette of the "Shadow the Time" clock suggests the shape of Resh, the "Horns Chair" that of Lamed, the "Italian Fish" armchair, Zade, the "Big Easy Volume 2" armchair, Shin, the

"Little Heavy" and "Double Take" chairs, Tet. The concave mirror surrounding the "Chair by its Cover" reminds us of Pe, an inverted U with a curious appendix hanging down inside. The "Looploop" chair is both a Gimel and a Mem, and the three chairs in the "Eight by One" series are reminiscent of Tet, Kaph and Lamed.

Calligraphic Architectures

This game of analogies could be pursued further, but the important thing to notice is that Ron Arad's designs are increasingly responses to calligraphic-type demands. His looping handwriting applies equally well to furniture and architecture. The 1992 "Looploop" armchair's thread-like profile is like the cord of a whip being cracked, an impression heightened by the material from which the seat is made, a mat of perfectly flexible woven steel wire which, in the "London Papardelle" version, extends down onto the ground like a rug that can be rolled up into a foot-rest.

Thus when, having founded "Ron Arad Associates" with Caroline Thorman and turned his back on the "One Off Showroom" in Covent Garden (whose atmosphere was described by Christine Colin as being like "a pre-historic cave re-worked by Robinson Crusoe"), in favour of "Chalk Farm Studios" in north-west London, opened in 1991, he began working in a very different space, in a very different spirit.

The same flowing curves were to be found everywhere, whether on the great rolling wave of the parquet floor or in the

2 R Not, 1992.
A black steel hollow box with four chairs cut into it in four different seating heights, from a high stool to a low armchair. The box can stand on any one of four different sides. The inset chairs are in mirror polished stainless steel.
(Collection of J & D Blackburn).
Design: Ron Arad
Ph: Christoph Kicherer

After Spring/ Before Summer, 1992.
A mirror polished stainless steel rocking daybed in one line, thick in the middle and thinning to the extremes. The small base is weighted with lead. With a sprung steel base.
Design: Ron Arad
Ph: Christoph Kicherer

giant white bat's wing of the ceiling, supported to the height of the flexible PVC windows by cut-out sheet-steel pillars, christened "Calligraphic columns" precisely because of their graciously slender, curving outlines.

Arad has developed his skilfully-inflected calligraphy in the vast context of the New Tel Aviv Opera, giving each space its own particular character by the use of different materials. The bronze-cloured wall of the bookshop is like a series of flexible straps in the process of being lashed energetically but frozen in mid movement, one above the other. The ceiling of the auditorium is a dark sheet with holes of light in, up towards which rise, without distorting it but rather as if to stress its immateriality, slanting posts in yellow, shining bronze. The bar surfaces are faced in the same woven stainless steel wire that gives the chairs ("Looploop", "London Papardelle", "Looploom", "Up Like a Bear" and others) much of their strange beauty, echoing their flexibility but also connecting with the semi-transparent honeycomb of the "Deep Screens". The most unusual part of this extraordinary set-up is the reception area, a concrete ribbon structure traversed by a staircase that Arad calls "The island". Everything there is based on a play of cut-out and intersecting shapes which brings a speculative richness to their descriptive geometry, producing a remarkably expressive space. Thus the staircase is the result of interpenetrating, rippling volumes sliced horizontally and displaced vertically in relation to each other. The ribbon of concrete, for its part, has been pierced by cylindrical and conical forms which, now removed, have left behind a series of curious loop-holes. Arad used a similar technique, but reversed, in the transparent, parallelepipedic space which crowns the "Y Building" constructed in the

Korean capital in 1995: there, the penetrating forms, standing out in bright colours, are suspended in the void.

Ideas Materialise, Intentions become Experiments...

These experiments with volumes intersected by surfaces or by other volumes are among Ron Arad's favourites. The ways in which he exploits sectioned profiles in his furniture have already been mentioned. But equally admirable is the mastery with which he uses cut-outs, retaining only the structural elements and making the sectioning process yield subtle ridged designs.

That is what he does with "2 R Not", a strange four-position chair constructed in 1992, which also raises the question of Arad's conception of the relationship between a "useful" object and its user. The parallelepipedic volume can be positioned in relation to each of its surfaces, four of which are useful in that they each offer a different seating position. This shows an attention to ergonomics like that found in the "Rover" seat, but also, and above all, a desire to have other people share his enthusiasms. When it comes to the search for greater comfort, Arad knows that he is working with very relative notions. The most "ergonomically" designed seat can become thoroughly uncomfortable after a time, once it starts to be compressed by the sitter's weight, whereas a hiker who sits down on a rock at the edge of the path, or a child astride a branch in a tree, never complains of being uncomfortably seated.

In fact, what Arad is offering are materialised ideas, intentions to investigate and import into one's own life, in a total complicity

A Suitable Case.
A tight fit ply crate for a narrow "London Papardelle". The crate is a chair and is available separately.
Design: Ron Arad

between the designer, his created object and the recipient who, for his or her own pleasure, has adopted them both. People therefore play with his objects and explore them, getting to know them intimately in an intentionally changing physical relationship. So it was that Arad invented a seat that can be used in several positions, by simply turning it over.

"2 R Not" is a fine example of this, but "Creature Comfort", "Up Like a Bear", "Double Take, no Duckling no Swan and Soft in the Head", also from 1992, show the same intention. Arad also devised a conceptually simple form of mechanisation based on ratchets and torsion springs which allowed the seat height, and the tilt of seat and back, to be adjusted. The result was "Box in 4 Movements" (1994). He also re-thought the way his tipping seats work, giving them a small range of movement (the "After Spring" and "Looploom" chaise longues) but also taking into acount the danger that they might tip up completely, a risk cleverly avoided by judicious positioning of the user's centre of gravity, and the use of end-stops ("Rolling Volume", "Spanish Made"), or a counter-weight which made the seat behave like a self-righting wobbly toy, as in the case of the "A.Y.O.R." chair.

When a Ribbon of Steel is a Structure, and a Wavy Line Geometry...

The very special flavour of Arad's recent researches also comes from his imaginitive exploration of all the possibilities of flexible sheet steel. This process began to a certain extent with the "Well Tempered Chair" of 1987, but in 1991 Arad took daring to new limits with his highly ludic family of chairs and chaise longues, such as "Beware of the Dog", mounted on rings made out of bands of sprung flexible steel.

Then his attention turned from chairs to bookcases. Spiral or zigzag in shape, fitted with spacers or hanging brackets to act as end-pieces, strips of steel became standing or wall-mounted shelving units which, pliant but strong, flexed under the weight of their books. Arad's most recent bookshelves are great hoops of steel and glass which appear to roll around the house, their shelves kept horizontal by a special mechanism reminiscent of certain unicycles of the last century. This shift from sinuous line to an absolute geometricalisation close to the constructivism of a Moholy-Nagy or the concrete art of a Max Bill, marks a radical change indeed. It represents above all an assertion of the primacy of ideas over images, which can never be more than the free expression of an idea.

The Art of Interpreting Tradition to Give it a New Lease of Life

A master of metaphor (as the titles of his works demonstrate), Arad has never been afraid to muddy his tracks, or rather let them criss-cross with each other, while at the same time breaking traditional taboos. Once again, a reference to a predecessor illuminates his own practice. Whenever the work of Gerrit Rietveld is mentioned, one tends to think of the rigorous geometrical order of the De Stijl movement, characterised by a certain immobility and a hieratic tendency. Arad, though, sees Rietveld as a man with a love

This Mortal Coil, 1993.
Free standing book shelves. Blackened tempered steel strip coiled to form a spiral.
Form retained by partitions thru rivettes hinges. The hinges allow the coil to move in
a sprung action.
design: Ron Arad,
ph: Christoph Kicherer

of new ideas, carried away with the possibilities offered by new materials, and also much taken by things that move (see the arrangement of mobile partitions in the Schröder House). So, for Arad, the "Zigzag" seat, which does away with verticality, becomes a symbol of movement. Hence, his "Rietveld chair" of 1991 has at its back a pliant arc of steel which allows it to flex and, if tipped backwards, to turn into a flexible chaise longue.

There is doubtless a degree of humour, but certainly no irony, in this free interpretation of a mythical object, a reworking which rather reflects Arad's interest in the *œuvre* of an illustrious predecessor who, in the 20s and 40s was already making armchairs (the ancestors of the "Well Tempered Chair") from sheets of fibrous material or aluminium simply cut out, folded, bent into shape and lightly fixed together. *"The first step on the road to consciousness is awareness of existence as an individual, which starts with the separation of the self from the space around it"*, wrote Rietveld. His observation is especially relevant to pieces such as "Chair by its Cover", "2 R Not", "Appropriate" and even "Equal Partners", in which two users inside the same parallelepipedic volume are unable to see each other, and even more so to "A Suitable Case" and "And the Rabbit Speaks", in which space has become so private that the seats are at times encased in a box which is closed up again after use, and which is also a chair in its own right.

It is also a fine way to make a chair like "Schizzo" look unique. This is one of those objects specially designed by Arad for limited edition reproduction. Without wishing to make what may seem an over-hasty generalisation, it could be said that, designed with simplicity in mind, these objects all escape the trap of repetitiveness through their profound originality. If "One Off" was designed, in his "Kee Klamp" period, as a sort of laboratory allowing made-to-measure pieces to be turned out on demand, it later became a way of building prototypes, also on demand, of registered designs which would then be subject to the vagaries of hand-crafted production. When companies like Vitra AG or Moroso consider producing Ron Arad's furniture, the realities of the industrial process need to be taken into account. The "Well Tempered Chair" or "Schizzo" lent themselves to this quite well, but to fit the requirements of the Spring Collection the "Big Easy" armchair needed to be re-interpreted, losing its metallic coldness to become "Big Soft Easy", a chair cut out of a large block of soft expanded polyurethane and covered in felt.

Like a Jester with his Hat in the shape of Infinity...

In the space of a few years, Ron Arad has become one of the superstars of international design. Galleries, annual and triennial fairs all fight to ensure his presence. He has become a well-known personality, his silhouette easily recognisable as he sweeps by in his long coat and hat with, on occasion, tastefully-placed holes in...

When I see him I am forcefully reminded of the image of the Jester, the first Major Arcanum in the Tarot pack, a street acrobat and artisan surrounded by symbolic objects, the precious tools which he uses to call into being the marvellous.

He too wears a hat whose broad brim is shaped like the algebraic sign for infinity, a potent symbol of the triumph of the mind. This same sign is cut out from the concrete ribbon of the foyer in the Tel Aviv Opera by a mysterious, imaginary cylinder. A magical perforation like those in the hat of Ron Arad, that astonishing magician constantly inventing new tricks who will continue to amaze us for a long time to come.

Why bark if you have a dog?

*T*his is the mould... this is the mould. Still hot. It's still hot for, like, three days after. Five hundred degrees. Doesn't it look like Marcel Duchamp's *pissoire*?

We were inspecting all versions and states of the vacuum-chair. There was a Japanese guy with us, very eager to learn. Fine, deconstructed clothing, katogan. Nobody seemed to know whether he was a journalist/photographer, a gallerist, a dealer, or an industrialist. He would ask acute questions, then crawl on the floor to shoot photos of the chair from underneath, or climb on another chair to get a bird's eye view.

Where's Dara?

We did a job and I had a big table with circles, and I wanted to find a chair to go with it, something based on concentric circles. Then we analyzed how we could have it stacked. The first ones did not have any drawings on them, but the circles were very important. I wanted them moiré. Then Domus called and asked: "can you design a totem for the center of Milan?" And I thought that might give us a chance... always wanted to do something in vacuum-formed aluminium. You saw the airplane wing in my kitchen. That was done by that factory and I'd said: we must be able to do furniture like this. But it is too expensive: the mould itself is expensive and so is the process. It takes twenty minutes to heat the plate before you can sssssttt suck it. And twenty minutes by the standards of my production, which is very artisanal, is fast, it takes two weeks to do a «Big Easy». But for commercial distribution, it's too long, because injection-molding is tss-tss-tss-tss, not twenty minutes. But Domus had a budget for a sculpture, I used the budget to invest in the tool to make the chair. The chairs that we have, the 500, it's a bonus. 500 chairs with a story to them - the opportunity to use this technique that I'd wanted to use for a long time came from the Domus sculpture. I proposed to them a realistic sculpture. Art financing design. When is a flag a flag, and when is a flag a painting? You know the Jasper Johns thing. Are the chairs in the sculpture still chairs? I' d played with this idea a little bit. The totem had to incorporate some sort of an information panel. I wanted to totally integrate it in the totem. Is a pixel-board still a chair? It was difficult to find someone who'd do a tri-dimensional pixel-board not on a rectilinear grid. I mean, in theory, when you think about it, it's the easiest thing in the world. But the biggest company which makes pixel-boards, Solari in Udine, which does all the message boards in airports, declined: sorry we cannot do it. Then Phillips said: we'll do it. They sent us to some people who work for them, near Malpensa, subcontractors, two people. When we went to see them, we didn't believe that they would be able to make it: they had a hi-fi shop that sells Phillips stuff, stereos, videos. So we went

Schizzo Chair, 1989.
One chair that splits into 2 almost identical chairs or 2 almost identical chairs that unite into one chair.
Design &Ph: Ron Arad.

there, Barnaby and me. OKay can we see your workshop? No. It's in another town. Can you do it? Yes. You're not worried about the job? You've got only two weeks. No, we're not worried. When they delivered, they said: you remember when you asked us if we were worried? Remember we said no? We lied. It was at the last minute on the morning of the installation, after a long night. We were not sure whether we'd get the pixel-board or not. But Barnaby had gone to the place where they work, and he called and said: I saw it. It's fantastic.

Back to the chairs. This company in Worcester makes things mainly for airplanes. It's a very good company, not typically English. In England they're usually bored: no, no, we can't do that. There, it was: yes yes, let's do it, tada. They came here to work with their computer. They use the same program that Frank Gehry is working on, Katia from Dassault, you take the same drawing drawn by the computer to the machine and it makes the mould. The mould, six tons of steel, was cut by one finger, dggiiiiiiii, in three weeks. The computer drawing can be inserted into a CNC machine to cut the mould, or, a plotter to produce a virtual reality print-out.

Funny thing is, my friend the painter who did the invitation - you see, I've a painting at home, with holes - he's sort of my best friend and he's doing these new paintings, huge, like this window. He came from Jerusalem and he showed me these paintings. It was unbelievable, six metres from here to here, and he had no idea of what I was working on and I had none either. And I saw this and I said: look at this. The similarity is amazing.

The mould takes six weeks to cut. We had a choice between a male and a female mould. We ended up with a female after a lot of considerations. Yeah. When we're done with the 500 chairs, I want to get this mould.

Also another thing - in the old days... Okay this is the drawing we made for the pixel-board...the director of Domus, Burckhardt, his job is to get money and have people to sponsor his products, so he negociated something with Vitra for the totem. In the meantime we're doing the chair with Vitra, the commercial version, the smaller one. They sent me the first mould, the one for a mock-up, because the injection-mould is a lot more expensive than the mould for vacuum-forming. For vacuum-forming you only need a male or female, for injection, you need two.

The press is some 1000 tons. The Japanese guy knows everything about it: he has visited the Vitra factory outside of Milan (!).

So before we do the injection moulded chair, we have to do several prototypes to make sure it's perfect. So we make a mould out of a material called plastic-wood. Same process as the steel, but a lot faster. Then they can do fiberglass very much like this material to check the comfort. You have something that you can try out, you can see. It's three centimetres smaller each way. You can try it.

Ahhh, says the Japanese tester leaning back in the chair.

Another thing is, you have this thickness in the seat and gradually it gets thinner so it's softer. We had a carbon-fiber version and we

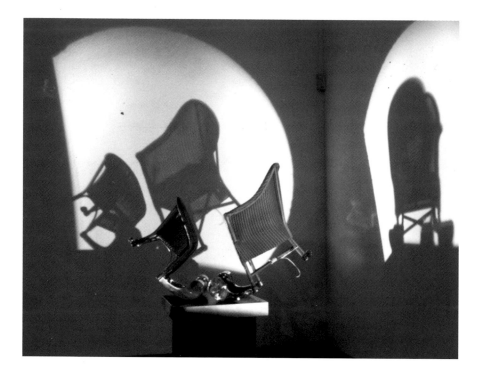

Looming Lloyd, 1990
A pair of clamp on "shoes" shift the weight of the chair so that the chair is looming when not in use. The shoes can be clamped to any 4-legged chair.
design Ron Arad

took it to make the mould for this. There might end up being real competition between the Vitra and the Kartell chair. They will come on the market at the same time. What I like when I see people sitting on this is that it's like a group of people wearing the same skirt...

In the carbon-fiber one, the most expensive element is the material itself. So I asked: what do you do with the off-cuts, what do you do with the waste? Well, they said, we throw it away once a week. So I had a chair entirely made out of the waste, so the material is free. Then they said to me: can we make one? Well... I said. We'll give it to the most artistic worker. No I said, please give it to the least artistic one. So anyway, they made one and I did not like it too much. Somebody had tried to organize the pieces. Want to see it? Tada-tada. Looks very patchwork. I did not want to show it in the exhibition: it looked too much like another arty chair. If only it had been... without any attempt to do art...it could have been fantastic. It has great potential. Absolutely free. And the mould is made: so what's the problem? All these rejects in twenty years, will be the most expensive things. So we have this room here where we show it without really showing it. With some survivors going back six years. Then I decided not to make any of these pieces here and started with Stefano. He does them perfect. I did not want to get into the situation where somebody tries to imitate the early «One Offs». This is the way it was, this is the way it became, Monsieur, and that's it. Finished. We cannot produce anymore.

Later there would be the usual Italian quartet, three males + one female, coming on purpose from a remote provincial town, looking reasonably well-to-do and enthusiastic about the work. They'd asked for a special contribution. Already had a fine design collection (Sottsasses and Mendinis and, yes one Ghini), a noble cause (their corporate cultural identity), but they would pay for the shipping. Yes. Ron could be certain that he would benefit greatly from his own generosity. And they would pay for his ticket. Yes.

I was born in Tel Aviv. My mother was from Bulgaria. She did not come from an art milieu. She came from a very poor family. She grew up around Tel Aviv where she was brought when she was three years old. There was a small Bulgarian community, Ladino-speaking. They had been kicked out of Spain in 1492. So she spoke this very special Jewish Ladino, a language that came from Spanish. She did not speak Bulgarian.

We were going to Sofia. We had been through a divine Hungarian putza sunset. When we got to the Yugoslavian border, they wouldn't let us in. So what! We'd cross Romania instead. At three a.m. we drove silently through the city of Arad. Frankly, it did not look like so much fun.

She doesn't come from a very cultured family, but she was the youngest and the freak: she could draw, so she was specially protected as the gifted one. My mother's talent just sucked her out of her natural surroundings. She was, and still is, an obvious talent. She grew up as a painter in the times when French painting was ruling the world. You had to go to Paris, lead the bohemian life in Montparnasse. Tatata-tatata. The French painting that she was exposed to was pretty much post-impressionistic, not abstract.

Thick paint, patches of colours and the like. It required a set of techniques and codes. My mother knows the rules of composition, what is correct and what is not. She is a fantastic draughtsman: even today, she can go anywhere with watercolors and do a landscape as a virtuoso. My father on the other hand, came from Russia. He went to school in Vienna, much more cultured - he knew the complete works of Shakespeare and he could speak Latin... He turned into a good expressionist sculptor. Then he ran into my mother... some people warned her that he would upstage her, but she did not pay attention. In fact it was him who quit and threw all his works off the cliff (some of them actually survived still). He quit for a long time. Later, he came back with photography. He does exhibitions, very fresh and juvenile. Recently he has started computers and he combines the computers with photographic techniques. In his retirement from art, he has been very supportive to my mother. He could have become bitter. In fact he has become her best advocate. But he had sort of a wall against the avant-garde. I think she would have been better off without it. He takes care of her framing, of the transportation of her exhibitions and things like that. He is great support.

Wine or beer? Beer first? The place was Italian. We had beer all the same, Nastro Azzuro, per piacere.

As a kid I was very much aware of the whole scene. There were exhibitions and openings, where all the cousins came from small villages wearing their best shirts. It is a very provincial place,

Michelle Mabelle Milano Mon Amour, Milan, 1994. Detail of Interior.
Design: Ron Arad Associates
Contractor: Marzorati Ronchetti.
Ph: Alberto Piovano

Israel has a very small and close-knit artistic community. The artists all know each other. And this community was sort of around me. Everytime I drew, my mother would say: oh he's going to become an architect (a safer position, she thought, than artist, as it combines artistic sense with function, good sense and utility). My brother on the other hand had no visual talent whatsoever. He's a musician. Maybe it is the youth art camps, the art-loving summer camps that did it. There was drama, music, photography, painting, sculpture, all people like fourteen years old for one month...it came with socializing, sex, culture, rock'n roll...all my friends, some of them I still see now, went to these places. I have to admit now that these places sort of worked. It was formative. You had to pretend to know things you didn't know. At that time, I would come back and argue with my father about Schoenberg and Bartok. My father believes in debating and of course to do so, you can't be of the same opinion. Otherwise there is no point. My father was a Communist in his youth and I became in my youth, more left-wing than he was and more avant-garde. But generally we remained on the same side. My friends would go home to a different planet, and developed through conflict. I did not have that.

I remember when Le Corbusier died and it was a big thing. Others, Martin Luther King, the Kennedys. And I saw the films of Norman McLaren and Calder's films and tadatada...and I knew of Black Mountain College and John Cage. Very early. Because it's provincial. When I came to the A.A., I was shocked by how uninformed the students were. Because when you are from the centre, you don't need to work on information. It happens to me now when I go to remote places and they know more about what I do than people who live here and even more than myself.... They rely on magazines and whatever information they can get and they do look for it. They dig it up.

So what kind of æsthetics had shaped him? Obviously he was not on Mondrian's side. Not even on Malevitch's.

More on Kiesler's, I guess. But, I'm not aware of how it started. When I was at the A.A., there was that mood: nobody was into building. Me, I could draw, do paperwork. But I was very lazy. I am not a labourer. I am not a methodical person. I'd never spend my time at a drawing board. I used to draw staircases but I never went into any measuring. I was a very reluctant architecture student. There were times when I thought of myself as a Bob Dylan. I played the guitar. I could entertain friends. Played the blues Boooo-boooobooo...but then I realized that I was not good enough, that I'd reached an area where... I was interested in 60's music. Give me Lennon, give me Dylan, take away... then give me Duchamp, Marcel D. and take Breuer, Marcel B. I always was an outsider to the architecture world. I tried to adopt heroes: Scharoun and the Philarmonic, the Corb of Ronchamp, Kiesler, Prouvé for common sense. It is not one or the other. As far as Black Mountain College was concerned, I was on Rauschenberg's and Twombly's side. As I said, I am not a methodical guy. So Albers... I am lazy. That's why I do so much. I jump from one thing to the other. I am not into things to be absolutely solved and resolved.

The New Tel Aviv Opera. View of cafe from opening in spiral wall.
Architects: Ron Arad/ Alison Brooks Ron Arad Associates
Ph: G. Dagon

Strict Family, 1991
Like the "Eight By One" hollow constructions with tempered steel "bones" the three
cantilever types are joined by a fourth that has a sprung loop at the back. The sides
of the chairs are polished stainless steel and all the rest is black steel.
design Ron Arad
ph: Howard Kingsnorth

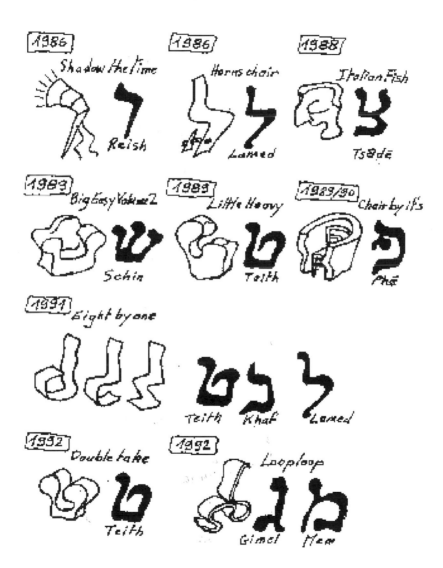

A Language of Forms Rooted in Ancient Hebrew Writing
drawing : Raymond Guidot

Take the welded pieces. It was so rough to weld. The pieces came perfectly rough. Then as it got better, they couldn't stay half-way between rough and finished. So they had to become perfectly finished. The whole point of them at first was the roughness. Later it was the perfection. Like Leigh Bowery said, speaking to a fashion designer: if a skirt was short, it had to be shorter. If it was tight, it had to be tighter. It is the same with the polished weldings.

So Bluesy-Blue-Collar Arad went into welding. In the heart of the sparkling darkness of the workshop, masked as a young Hephaïstos having borrowed Medusa's head from Perseus, B.B.C.A. would distort and assemble metal. Whether rough or perfected, the shapes would take watchers off guard. From cavern's walls to knight's armours, from archaic to medieval (and a little computer chip for the road), they would confuse and blurr and drive critics amok. How would you label those big fragments of warriors, not even standing, erect as the terra-cottas of the first emperor of China, but kneeling, rolling around the floor? B.B.C.A. seduced England through its own intimate weakness, not displaying any "silence, exile and cunning" but simple extravaganza and a zest for tragedy. Years back, my friend Lewis Baltz and I attended a performance of Macbeth *in Manaus. The opera-house must have had something to do with it: a Scala clad in pink stucco and topped by a ceramic dome, right in the middle of nowhere. Amazonia. So exotic. The temperature was 95° Farhenheit outside and 98° inside the house. Humidity was 90 % on both sides. Those barbarians straight out of the frozen mists of Scotland, wore black leather biker's outfits. The battle scenes were choreographed half-way between the Tokaido and Sherwood forest, samouraïs and Robin Hood's companions and those long wooden sticks could certainly break your skull. From the bloody hands scene on, Lady Macbeth wandered on the stage bare-chested. Now and then, bats would come out of the flies for a tentative dive to the pit. Fffrrrightning! Despite (or because of) those obvious displacements, the production was utterly convincing and, yes, beautiful.*

The Roverchair was done in my first place in Covent Garden. There I had a big space, a big, empty shell to do something with. Because of the architecture, I had to do things for the place. What I did first was a big table five metres long like an ironing board which would swing here and there. I used to sit on the edge and swing and people would say don't swing, it is not strong enough. I'm saying this because it was not until the next place that I had a chance to do real architecture. The Council was to demolish the place for further developing. So I was sort of free to do whatever. I had two floors. So I punched a big hole in the ground and made a big staircase to go to the basement. I did it out of concrete and incorporated a device linked to a synthetizer into each step : as you walked down the stairs it played music, synthesized music, which kept changing at random. At first I tried to use a device with needles like the old record players. It worked but it was not too reliable. Then I found detectors which were part of a sophisticated alarm system. They were very sensitive to any vibration and would translate it to a huge synthesizer, with the power of about four big orchestras. It was a big sound system Baa-Ba-Boo-Booboo-Booom-Shrieeek..

So you would go down the steps and it played a tune or rather a series of sounds which it never could play twice. People went downstairs and came back up and they would say: excuse me, can I buy the tape you're playing?

So we ended up making those concrete synthesizers with a concrete base and a horn. People wanted to have the music: I could not sell the tapes... less the stairs! So I sold them the instrument. We must have made six of them or so. Somebody came to the studio recently and said, you know I have bought one of your synthesizers. I was very jealous of him.

Lunch and dinner, we would go next door. Belgo. Entrance: rusted, steel gangway and Ron's interpretation of the bottom of a cargo in the O'Neil (Eugene) style with biiiiig aluminium contorted pipes. Then, schizophrenia: would you contemplate Ron's side from the other side or would you prefer to sit on Ron's side and forget the rest? "Twas easy to forget it all: they passed Belgian style, a long rack of wood with little glasses of booze, (une fois!) both sides.

To cast the figures in the Gaultier boutique I used the prototype of something I thought would make me rich (it didn't). It was called the "Transformer". It's like the Sacco with little spheres of polystyrene and an air-tight envelope with a valve. When you suck the air out through a hoover, it becomes hard as a brick,

Adidas Sport Café, Toulon, 1996.
Detail of mirror polished stainless steel bar with raised mirrored steel "satellites".
design: Ron Arad Associates

The New Tel Aviv Opera. Spiral wall of island with crush bar in foreground.
Architects : Ron Arad/Alison Brooks, Ron Arad Associates.
Ph: G. Dagon

then it becomes soft again when you let air back in. So it was the instant customer's chair. It gets hard as a package of coffee, you know Lavazza, except that it takes your shape. We suspended production, though, because it was too fragile to fire and scratches. And it cost about 100 pounds to make at the time, and between smokers and cats... I'm ready to do it again with better envelopes. We had produced a few and some people still have them. It was the product of circumstances: I met a man through the yellow pages. The ad said: we can make anything out of plastic. So I met Dr Victor who was seventy-eight at the time. That was somewhere near Waterloo, but we soon discovered that he lived near me. From that day, I talked to him everyday until he died at eighty-two. It was an instant friendship. He never sent us invoices. He made these things for me and he refused to be paid. He wanted to make a contribution, he said. And at one point... in those days we had another partner, who was no good. Dr Victor bought the major share. We liked each other. He didn't have children. And I don't know why or how, but he became... when my daughter was born, we used to call him «honorary grand father». He was a big help, Doctor Eric Victor. When I did the piece for Dokumenta, I called it Doctor Victor. He was incredible. In the case of the "Transformer", we did not get further on it because in my usual way of doing it, I didn't try to refine: I just did it. By the way, some German company has asked Starck to do something with the principle and Starck was very good, he said: it belongs to Ron, I don't want to touch it...

With Doctor Victor we sort of checked on what was possible and how. He introduced me to this technique which is used for medical purposes, for transporting of people who are injured, without moving them, something like immobilizers; And he was making them for incidents in coal-mines and such. I said, look, let's make furniture out of it. He did it. He was all excited about doing something different. Well, yes, now that you mention it... I'd thought of Gaetano Pesce's Up & Up and the Sacco. But I'd never made the connection with the splints that Eames did early at his beginnings. But yes, it works.

Chalk Farm sits on the verge of something and doesn't know yet what. Quite deserted in the morning and you're lucky if you can get a Turkish English breakfast. Later, in the afternoons, people pour in slowly, stores open, mostly junk furniture, on the derelict storage side of the street, clothing on the other. Difference being: junk lies on the sidewalk, clothing is on hangers. The slow-wandering crowd exhibits a stroboscopic vision of all fads since 1959: Mary Quant, Hare Krishna, Sid Vicious, Johnny Rotten (it is not the same) and whoever, all parachuted in the latex epoch. Tattooes all over. And piercings: on lips, earlobes, necks, eyelids, cheeks, foreheads, and whatever you can think of, providing they are prone to leaving the pathetic little marks of the rites of passage to manhood/-womanhood. Moving. The studio is just off the crowd before the street sloooowly ascends to Belsize park.

Clock-light. I was visiting a show room, it had a sort of a patch on the ceiling and I said oh, they did a clock on the ceiling with a projection. Then I had a better look: there was no clock

Michelle Mabelle Milano Mon Amour, Milan
design: Ron Arad Associates, 1994
ph: Alberto Piovano

here Why did I think there was a clock here? But it gave me the idea. Then I went and did a clock with projected light. I called it "Shadow of Time".

Come to Milan, he'd said. Well, Okay. We went to see the show. Hobo Arad + Handsome Ingo. Nice pair. Good casting. There was a huge crowd awaiting the disclosure of the gates. Rushed into the courtyard and zoomed to the show room. HA and HI were there. They would talk to everybody, patiently explaining the whats, whys and hows of whatever. The vacuum-moulded chairs were all over the place, the special painted ones well aligned, most of them already sold to avid collectors. HI had done something simply brillant, a bulb with a hologram inside or something of the kind. Magic, they all gasped (is there any magic left? It all seems so natural. But we're early devotees of Telsa's and Byron the Bulb's, right?). There were also unfinished protos of the chair, still uncut, blooming like rose-trees before trimming, more beautiful even than the chair itself. One of them, everybody knew. It looked exactly like the others scattered in the room. It was set by the biiiig table. But the whole crowd seemed to be aware: well, it did look suspicious. And the more you looked at it, the more banal and undistinctive you convinced yourself that it was, the more suspicious it became. Then there was the radiant one, whom everybody had spotted as the one, and he sat down on it. And the bolt, the slightly loose bolt, which until then had resisted restless fatties and nervous sissies, he knew him too. "Fatalitas!" it said to itself and gave in.

Later we played ping-pong. Regular HA's table, shapeless, tilted upward, rounded angles, chromed to kill. HA said: you play much better than me. He won. He always does.

Sicilian avenue was somebody else's place, the partner's whom Mister Victor helped us to disentangle ourselves from. But that was a survival thing. That was One Off first address. Next one was like a big studio. It had this shutter that you had to raise every morning. And this was Covent Garden. People could look in and see what I was doing. So I was «visible».from the very beginning And I used the place for parties and things. I did exhibitions. One was with Nigel Coates, Heads for "84. Took place in "83. We invited people to do full-size heads, figurative or otherwise. And they were displayed on pedestals. A sweet exhibition with people like Paolozzi, Terry Jones... and quite a wild party. We did an exhibition of Peter Wilson's too. Suddenly I was the first one from the A.A. that had found a place and a space in Covent Garden big enough to do things in. One time I had four Japanese people come in and say: "editor told us photograph party in One Off." I said: sorry but we don't have a party. When we have a party... give us your address and we'll invite you. You'll come and photograph. Well, we go back to Tokyo wednesday. I said: look, sorry, but no. He said we buy drinks. I said: please. We're very...And he said: we pay 50 pounds each guest. And I said: actually we do have a party on wednesday. So we started calling people: hey come to a party you get 50 pounds. It was the funniest party ever. They brought the drinks, the food. And we did not believe the 50 pounds. But in the end, as people came out, they had a book of money from the

bank and clank, clank, clank. It was like «miracle in Milan». De
Sica's. I have to say that they had limited the number of guests.
Enough to photograph. And asked: where you buy your socks,
where you buy your pants, where you buy this and that? It was a
real job. And then things like that started happening. That's
another one. This comes from a commercial. For beer. When they
came to me, they came with a storyboard like bing-bang-bam.
We'd like to use the "Rover chair". Can we give you 5000 pounds?
Well... I said, Yeah Okay Would you like to be in the commercial?
And I said: no. But I still don't know if it's for beer or for the
"Rover chair". I don't know if it was good for the beer, but it was
good for me.

> *We sat and skimmed through breviaries of the good ole 80's*
> *with bemused desolation. All those pretty colored cartoons*
> *drawn by prepubescent Milanese designers under the protective*
> *gaze of their moms (it was a miracle at the time to find an*
> *apartment in Milan and mamma would keep on cooking the*
> *pasta and ironing shirts forever anyway). We would ask,*
> *whatever happened to this person or that one: family life or*
> *family business, car crash, heroin, AIDS, self-denial, Toto-*
> *calcio? Their hour of fame had lasted 15 minutes (if that) then*
> *swept away, forever forgotten. Ciao.*

The metal thing might have started just because for two years
on Shelton street we had no balustrade at all. I'd managed to get it
approved by the authorities. Then two years later, some guy from
the Public Health and Safety Works came to me: some other guy

The New Tel Aviv Opera. View showing Foyer Bookshop in foreground with waiting area under cantilevered auditorium volume and spiral wall in background.
Architects : Ron Arad/Alison Brooks.
Ph: G. Dagon

Adidas Stadium, Paris
Computer image showing video monitor.

wanted to do the same in another place in Covent Gardens and could not and said what about...?. So ahhh. I went to court. And the judge said: why don't you do something tubular? After all, you're famous for your tubes... I lost anyway. So I said Okay I'll do it for you: the tube was zero in diameter down here and one metre up there. This was my first welded piece. This is when I learned first. Shortly after that, there was an exhibition at the Serpentine and I converted the balustrade into the Horn, and then Shelton street was a real welding course on the walls. The windows I just blew holes into with the torch. I liked it. It's one shot. And I wrote with the torch on the walls: heart and design, falling water, hommage to illegible, blue daylight, then streams of consciousness, my name in Hebrew, all sorts of funny things. Everything had to be invented.

There was a party at the studio. The Milan show had moved. Very different from the way it was, much closer, more intimate. Ingo and Ron exchanged glances. Accomplices in crime: the soft "bricolage" + high technology connection. Do-it-yourself... if you can. There were beers in the courtyard. The Citroen Maserati which usually sits there (belonging to one of Ron's computer wizards. Whose else?) was not on display that night. Later it would rain, discreetly, as if to remind you where you were.

The first company I designed for was Vitra. I had read an article in Blueprint, one of the first issues, about Rolf Fehlbaum. There was a picture of the "Rover chair", part of his collection. I didn't know who he was. They say he's the man who loves chairs. And he is quoted as saying that I'm one of the artists... so I say, Okay, alright. Then he starts the Vitra collection. And he has all the rights for Eames, so he does not need to go to Milan every year and exhibit whatever new products. He has a winner already. And he's done Bellini, Citterio, and they sell. But Felhbaum wanted to go beyond. Then he invited in Pesce, Sottsass, Artschwager and Scott Burton, another artist from N.Y. , he's dead now - check him out, furniture as sculpture - and myself. So when Vitra comes to and says, can you please design a piece for edition... So I started with Vitra having a big factory, fifteen hundred skilled workers, they can do anything... and then I could not go beyond doing something that I could do myself. My skill was my chain and ball. So I did for them, something that I could have done for myself, so it was a waste of time... in a way. In another way, it's one of my favourite pieces. Because it's a very easy, portrait of a chair. Like a Matisse portrait, just four lines. And yet you can't argue that it's not a chair. It's an armchair. It was the time Starck did the Richard III chair and I saw some connection there. I love the Richard III chair. Wooong. I like being jealous. And it made me jealous. I came up with this, maybe in some kind of distant conversation with Richard III. Same generic thing. Well... I knew it was to be reasonably comfortable, it had to be. But I did not know it would be so different sitting in it than in any other chair. I really would have forgiven it for not being so... just Okay say... but when you sit in it for the first time, or when you watch people sit on it...Tttsshhee. We talked about doing a new edition of it with Vitra. Now, for some reason it's getting more in demand.

Bridge stretches from "hill" to mezzanine office. Contains office heating ducts and provides furniture display.
Design : Ron Arad/Alison Brooks.
Ph: Christoph Kicherer

But it was on every possible magazine as soon as it was done. So...

In fact it's the very first metal chair but it has no welding at all. Just clippings and the natural shape of the material: harmonious shapes. The welding I was forced into by law. So I called someone who worked in Brighton. He came with his equipment. A young guy. That's how I started out welding: it was the first piece of a mass formed by just the skin. And the difference between the tempered and the welded steel is that the well-tempered has no memory: you bend it and it springs back. The mild steel that I use for the welded pieces, you bend and it stays. You just hammer the plate and use the welding as a fixative. Tchou-tchou-tchou.

And unlike what you might think, this is not a decor. When you make this and put a chair in it, you think for a second and you know you don't need to make that one. There are enough chairs around. So you just pick one and this envelope out of stainless steel, mirrored so it distorts it, and reflects it endlessly. The chair is the subject matter. It becomes endless as you walk around; it changes and doubles and reflects almost as a kaleidoscope. I made two: on this one, I wrote on why bark when you have a dog? And on the other one was, why have a dog if you can bark? I mean, why make a chair? We don't need any...

Did he mean that at a certain point his activity was probably more compulsive than rational? That it was only some "Kunstwollen", some irrepressible will to make?

There is not anything else. You don't really need us. This was a sort of comment on the state of things. We had become very good at welding by that time. To the point where we became bored. We did it for a long time until we were taken up by the Italians. One day, the Italians came here and they bought the studio to carry on the welding work. So we stopped. They produce dozens a year maybe. And they get the new design, like the Cartier Foundation tables. Everything I do that is not for mass-production.

After doing things myself for a long time, I thought it was better not to do so much or else I might become like a glass-blower, someone with a skill, churning out more and more.

The book-worm existed as a studio piece in its own right. There was a moving free standing piece - same steel as well-tempered, which has the same flexibility. Then there is the wall version. This is when I called Kartell and said: look, let's do it in plastic. The studio in Italy still produces them in metal. Me I don't make anything anymore. The first one was in my home. But no, I'm not a steel worker any-more. I'm white collar. There are eight of us here. I want to keep it on a small scale. I don't ever want to come to the point where it gets impersonal. I'm very lucky because I don't need to keep the archi-tecture jobs coming in. I don't depend on doing conversions or the like. We would say no. We're not interested. Here comes Caroline.

As it turned out, he was to be neither an architect, nor an artist, nor a designer, stricto sensu. How did he decide that he was not to be...

I never decided anything. It was not a decision. I did not know I would become a sort of furniture designer. I did what I could. I couldn't do the other things. It is not as if I had a grand scheme or a manifesto that design should be spontaneous and bababababa. It happened because I worked in London and I escaped from an architecture office. And there was no design scene in London, like say in Milan. It was a desert. So I had to invent. In Milan there was activity which produced things and made instant successes like Starck's. There was nothing equivalent here. I was sort of on my own, still needing my links with the ex-AA people. When I started doing the Rover chair, of course I knew about Picasso, Marcel Duchamp's readymades, but it was not about that and it was not a manifesto about recyckling either. Nothing to do with that. It had to do with something I could do. I was as conceited then as I am now. I had to come up with things to get people to say haaa haaa. The exhibition place was there and I had to provide for something in order to exist. Physically. I started doing things which I could do without too much effort. To take the Rover seat from the car, do the frame, was very little effort. I was smart enough not to stick to the same design. Then I had to do things physically myself. I had fun. And because I was lucky enough to have space at Covent Garden, and everything I did was very visible, lots of peolple came in and out. Covent Garden was like summer camp, the A.A., just another period of time. It was like, give me some money, I'll give you some designs. You had to deal with the public on a small scale. Then you learn business. Me, I had a whole year without doing any paperwork. Then it started building up. Can we see the receipts, they said. I don't have them,

Belgo Centraal, Covent Garden, Londres
architectes: Ron Arad/Alison Brooks
ph: Richard Davies

The New Tel Aviv Opera, Israel
View of Foyer Bookshop. Enclosure of bronze rods.
architect: Ron Arad/Alison Brooks
ph: Christoph Kicherer

I said. I was totally innocent to this type of things. I did eveything free-wheeling. I would sit in the studio on Saturdays and people would ask me to draw things for them out of the Kee Klamp system: all sorts of beds and storage things. They would come and say, we have this room and they had the measurements and they were happy that I would draw for them tatatata that place that they could identify as their room. Instantly. What you want. The Kee Klam was invented in 1932 by someone called Gascoigne, like the soccer player. Very versatile and coming in different finishes, bright colors, very smooth, like cars. So people came to me with photographs. I used to do the drawings, and I knew the kind of fittings to use, and I could give them the price instantly. And I would deliver. You want to mount it yourself or shall we do it for you? And so I started to have people working with me and Caroline joined to do the administration. And then I decided: basta with this system. I just didn't want to do it. I enjoyed the beginning, doing the funny drawings but then...

So I had to say Okay, what now?

So, I did pieces like the remote control light, the concrete stereo, all things that I could do myself, pouring the concrete, mixing the pebbles... I must have done about twenty-five of them. They still work. Somebody has three and refuses to sell us one. No. I can't even do another one. I can't. What do you do? Make concrete toasters, concrete telephones? You have to stop. The Rover chairs became our best selling thing. You could fill up every week. We could have become a Rover chair factory. When it was most popular, I decided to stop. We declared the last one hundred.

They were bought in two days. And that was it. Because it meant that you had to store the chairs, become a factory business. I never wanted to get big. I am very well protected here, very spoilt. But there are things that I need to do. Thank God for that. I've got to write about Rolf Fehlbaum for some New York... it'd better be good.

I know I have, for some reason, an aversion to conventions. Don't know where it comes from. But I am not an angry man. It's part of the same thing when I say I'm lazy. I have to make my mark by different means, not by hard work, not by slaving, not by tedium. For me, something which is too elaborate does not justify itself. How do you justify so much effort on something? The bigger the effort, the bigger the failure. If you don't try hard, if your trick is not to try hard, it's bound to be Okay. Ever since I was a kid, I have had the same trick: don't take yourself too seriously. Because if you do, you tend to be criticized seriously. I don't want that. I just want the easy way. I prefer truth to sincerity. Dylan says in one of his songs: to live outside the law you have to be honest.

Why have a dog if you can bark?

Chair of a Pedestal, 1991
collection "Spring" for Morosso, Italy.
design: Ron Arad

Biography

Born

Tel Aviv 1951, son of painter mother and photographer father

1971-73

Jerusalem Academy of Art and Architectural Association, London

1973

Moved to London

1974-79

Architectural Association - School of Architecture, studies under Peter Cook and B. Tschumi, contemporary of Nigel Coates, Peter Wilson and Zaha Hadid

1981

Established One Off Ltd. with Caroline Thorman in Covent Garden, London, a design studio, workshops and showroom.

First success with a range of furniture and interior structures in tube and clamps. Well known pieces include the "Rover Chair", the vacuum-packed Transformer" chair and the remote controlled "Aerial" light. Later work explored the use of tempered steel, first in the Well-Tempered Chair and laterin the popular "Bookworm".

1989

Founded Ron Arad Associates, Architecture and Design practice with Alison Brooks and CarolineThorman in Chalk Farm, London.

1993

One Off is incorporated into Ron Arad Associates.

1994

Ron Arad Studio established in Como in 1994 to continue and expand on theproduction of limited edition, handmade pieces as previously produced in the London workshops. The facilities of the Ron Arad Studio hugely expanded the possibilities in regard to materials, technique and engineering, allowing for such pieces as "Box in 4 Movements" (with a torsion sprung ratchet mechanism) or "R.T.W.", (a free-rolling large wheel with inner shelving that always remains parallel to the floor) to be produced.

Ron Arad was a guest Professor at the Hochschule in Vienna from 1994-7 and is currently the Professor of Furniture Design at the RCA in London.

Ron Arad was guest Editor of 1994 International Design Yearbook and Designer of the Year, 1994 and his work has been widely featured in many design/architectural books and magazines world-wide.

Furniture & Product Design

1986

Vitra International, Switzerland

Well-Tempered Chair - a tempered steel bouncy "skin-only" chair

Schizzo Chair - a single bent ply chair that can be pulled apart to form 2 separate chairs

A carbon-fibre expanding and contracting lightweight office daybed

An injection-moulding plastic low-cost stacking chair, an industrially produced version of the

Ron Arad Studio vacuum-formed aluminium chair.

1990

Moroso, Italy

Spring Collection - a range of 10 upholstered volume chairs/sofas, many a direct translation to a manufactured product from their handmade metal originals

Misfits - modular seating utilising ICI's environmentally friendly water-blown foam, Waterlily

Sof-Sof - a low seating system with inter-connecting slot-on elements to provide endless possibilities for seating arrangements

1991

Lippert Wilkins, Germany

Design of various desk-top accessories

1994

Draenert, Germany

> A long, low stainless steel sofa, the seat and back touching only at 3 points

1992

Noto, Italy

> Hotel Zeus - a mobile TV & video stand
>
> Anonymous - a range of stools, chairs and tables for café use

1989

Poltronova, Italy

> . A strip plywood table that extends from 1.5 metres to 3 metres

1993

Driade, Italy

> "Empty Chair" - plywood chair first developed for the Tel Aviv Opera.
>
> "Fly Ply" table - with 2 sets of legs - the hidden mechanism allows for either height of legs to be pulled down.
>
> "T44" - a mobile ply and aluminium folding trolley

1995

Fiam, Italy

> Cler - system of glass shelves and display units. The corrugated glass sides provide the channels for slotting in the various shelves and optional parts

1996

Martell, France

> A new flask bottle for a new colourless brandy aimed at a younger market. The bottle contains a floating laser-cut stainless steel label and a frosted lens topped drinking cup lid.

1996

Bigelli Marmi, Italy

> A table constructed from a single rectangular sheet of marble/aluminium lightweight composite. An entirely waste-free use of material

1996

Allia, France

> An ovoid shaped cantilevered double-skinned toilet

1996

Artemide, Italy

> Design & development of a lighting system exploiting reflection to create "virtual" light

1994

Kartell, Italy

Bookworm - a plastic industrial low-cost version of the Bookworm, in various lengths and colours. Currently Kartell's best selling productFantastic Plastic Elastic - a lightweight low-cost stacking dining chair in clear plastic with a double-barrel aluminium extruded structure A 1 metre diameter wheel containing shelving. The wheel can be rolled at will, the inner shelves always remaining parallel to the floor

1997

Alessi, Italy

Design & development of an efficient, minimal and almost invisible storage system for CD's

1997

Guzzini, Italy

Design & development of an extensive range of kitchen ware.

Architecture/Interior Design/Public spaces

Domus Totem, Milan 1997

A Totem commissioned by Domus magazine, for the centre of Milan. This totem is a "realistic" sculpture of a stack of 100 chairs in vacuum formed aluminium. The top chair carries a 3D live pixel board for transmitting messages. The chairs are discreetly welded to each other to form one structural unit. Some loose chairs are around the totem.

Private Residence, Israel 1997

Autonomous spatial elements and furniture for a newly built villa on a Mediterranean cliff. The main interior gesture is a pair of movable coves, smooth on the inside and ribbed with bookshelves on the outside.

14-15 Conduit Street, London 1997

Scheme for a 50 sm reception area in a newly refurbished office building.

Haverstock Hill, London 1997

Conversion of the top floors of a Victorian house to an open-plan and partially open air space.

Private Residence, London 1997

Located in a private, suburban street, this large family home is created by the overlap of two sheltering enclosures with an undulating terrace which extends the garden into the living rooms.

Mercedes Benz AG, Birmingham 1996

A proposal for the Mercedes Benz stand at the Birmingham Motor Show 1996. A unified total environment with elevated circulation grids around car 'arenas', mezzanine levels with backdrops of conical 'buildings' providing specialised enclosure.

Louisiana Museum of Modern Art, Denmark 1996

Concept and layout for British room in the Design and Identity Exhibition.

Adidas/Kronenbourg Sports Cafés, France 1996

The development of a concept for bar/restaurants equipped with state of the art, interactive A/V technology. The first Sport Café opened in Toulon, France in February, '97. A further seven cafés will be completed in major French cities by May '98.

Adidas Stadium, Paris 1995-96

The winning scheme in invited competition. The Adidas 'flagship' complex in the heart of Paris will be a 1300 sm total environment around the theme of sport, incorporating retail, interactive spaces, a cinema/auditorium, restaurants and cafés.

Art Gallery Competition, Walsall 1995

Two autonomous, inward-looking buildings along site boundaries, enveloping a courtyard between them, the courtyard roofed with a lens-shaped structure housing temporary exhibitions.

Galerie Achenbach, Dusseldorf 1995

Art Gallery with 8 x 4m long walls pivoting around structural columns. Double hinges enable an infinite number of gallery layouts.

Belgo Centraal, Covent Garden, London 1995

400 seat Belgian restaurant and Head Office.

Office 'Y' Building, Seoul, Korea 1995

A scheme for an international H.Q. in Seoul, Korea - in conjunction with David Chipperfield Architects.

Foyer Architecture, The New Tel Aviv Opera, Israel, 1989-1994

1200 sm four-storey, free form concrete structure within the Opera complex incorporating 200 seat restaurant, 5 bars, box office, book shop, amphitheatre and mezzanine. The project also comprises a 600 sm concrete volume forming the envelope of the 1500 seat auditorium. Completed October,1994.

Belgo Restaurant & Bar, London 1994

200 sm bar and restaurant extension. An open courtyard covered by a 70 sm glazed roof framed between a series of giant timber fins. A sinuous multi-level bar, a new 58 seat eating area, extensive food preparation facilities and a public beer store form part of the scheme.

Publishing Studio, Schopfhcim, Germany 1993

460 sm hill-side building in the Black Forest. Twin timber conical roofs of composite construction form 11-metre cantilevers from two supporting cores, dividing the building into a double-height studio and private living zone. A concrete retaining wall contains the library and services.

Michelle Mabelle, Milan 1994

Refurbishment of prestigious Via della Spiga fashion shop. Completed February, l994.

Vision for Vauxhall Effra Site, London 1994

Urban design and housing proposal for a riverside site comprising 17 storey apartment tower, low level housing, commercial and exhibition spaces.

Salon du Meuble de Paris, 1993

Exhibition design for the 4000 sm focus area to the Paris furniture fair.

Ron Arad Associates Studios, London 1991

Conversion of a derelict two-storey warehouse/courtyard building to gallery, architecture studio and workshops. A PVC roof membrane and expanded steel shell structure covers the 350 sm spaces below. Completed June,1991.

Château d'Oiron, France 1991

Entrance pavilion for the 16th century Chateau d'Oiron, centre for contemporary European art and sculpture in the Loire valley.

Philips Electronic Exhibition, Berlin 1990

Exhibition design incorporating Philips technology.

The Bureau Wapping -   Two level warehouse conversion into design studios.

Camomilla, Rome - Fashion shop in a historic building in Piazza di Spagna.

Equation, Bristol -   Department store for London fashion designers.

Milano Monamour, Milan - Fashion shop in Via della Spiga.

One Off Showrooms, Covent Garden- 1983,1986
Own studio and furniture showrooms in Neal Street and Shelton Street.

Bazaar, London 1984- Jean-Paul Gaultier fashion shop for women.

1 ◄

8 ▶

9 ▶

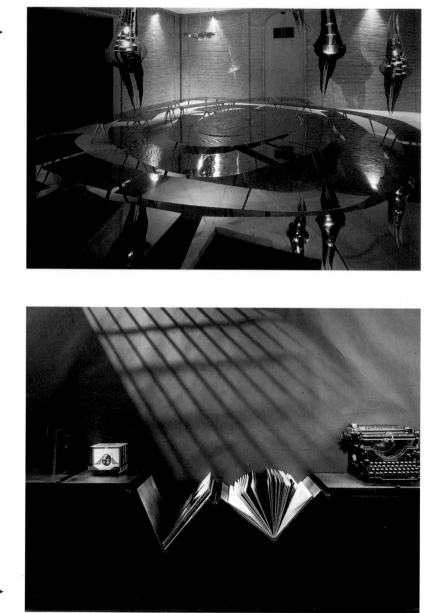

13 ◀

Selected exhibitions

1997

"Designed for Delight": Alternative Aspects of 20th Century Decorative Arts - Montreal Museum of Decorative Arts. Group international touring exhibition

Ron Arad and Ingo Maurer, Spazio Krizia

1996

Glasgow Festival of Architecture & Design

Ron Arad and Ingo Maurer, Spazio Krizia

1995

Museum of Applied Arts, Helsinki

Ron Arad and Ingo Maurer, Triennale, Milan

"Sticks and Stones", Vitra Design Museum, Touring Exhibition 1990-1995

1994

"L"Esprit du Nomade", Cartier Fondation, Paris

1993

"Breeding in Captivity" Edward Totah Gallery

"Design in the 20th Century", Grand Palais

"One Off and Short Runs", Centre for Contemporary Arts, Warsaw

1991

"A Break with Tradition", Gothenburg, Sweden

1990

Ron Arad Recent Works", Tel Aviv Museum of Art

1987

"Nouvelles Tendances", Centre Georges Pompidou

"Documenta 8", Kassel

Work in public collections

Vitra Design Museum, Weil am Rhein
Musée National d' Art Moderne/Centre Georges Pompidou, Paris
Fonds National d' Art Contemporain, Paris
Musée des Arts Decoratifs, Montreal
Metropolitan Museum of Art, New York
Victoria and Albert Museum, London
Stedelijk Museum, Amsterdam
Tel Aviv Museum, Tel Aviv

Bibliography

Bookworm, Volker Albus, Form Verlag, 1997

Keith Boxer, *Tensile Architecture in the Urban Context*, Publisher Butterworth, Heinemann, 1995

Ettore Sottsass, Cedric Price, *Ron Arad Associates: One Off Three*, introductions, Artemis Architectural Publications,1993

Samantha Hardingham, *London : A Guide to Recent Architecture*, Artemis,1993

Lucie Bullivant, *International Interiors 4,* Thames & Hudson, 1993

The International Design Yearbook 1993, dir. Ron Arad, Calmann & King, 1993

Alexandre Amato, *Engineering the Hi-Tech: The Architect's Guide to Production Engineering*, Oxford

John Beckmann, *Interior Details: Showrooms*, PBC International Inc. N.Y.

Carol Soucek King, *Architects and Designers Originals*, PBC International, 1993

Alexander von Vegesack, *Ron Arad*, Vitra Design Museum,Weim am Rhein, 1990

Deyan Sudjic, *Ron Arad Restless Furniture*, Fourth Estate & Wordsearch Ltd, London, 1989

Documenta 8 - Kassel 1987, Weber & Weidemayer GmbH & Co, Kassel, Germany, 1987

Peter Dormer, *The New Furniture*, Thames & Hudson, London, 1987

Nouvelles Tendances du Design, Les Avant-Gardes de la fin du XXe siècle, éditions du Centre Georges Pompidou, Paris, 1986.

John Thackera & Jane Stuart, *New British Design*, Thames & Hudson, 1986.

Cahiers du CCI Design: Actualités fin de siecle, Jean Mathey, Centre Pompidou/CCI, Paris, 1986

Contemporary Landscape from the Horizon of Postmodern Design, National Museum of Art, Kyoto, Japan, 1985

Uta Brandes & Michael Erloff, *Design Als Gegenstand*, 1984

Color Photograph Index

1: "R.T.W.", 1996.
A series of free-spinning wheels in various sizes. The shelves locked within the wheel always remain level with the floor while the outer wheel can be rolled at will.

2: "Adidas Stadium", Paris.
Computer image showing interior.

3: "Adidas Sport Café", Toulon, 1996.
Early computer image, bar area with large projection screens above for group viewing of events.
Ticker-tape scrolling display of latest sporting results.

4: "Un-Cut", 1997.
A low, untrimmed version of the aluminium vacuum-formed Tom Vac chair. Anodised in various colours. Polished stainless steel frame.
Ph: Wilhelm Moser

5: "Soft Heart", 1991.
Part of Spring Collection for Moroso, Italy.

6: Chalk Farm Studios, London. 1989.
A PVC roof membrane and expanded steel shell structure covers 350 sm of space below.

7: "Y" Building, Korea, 1995.
A group of autonomous, movable structures within the 9-metre high space for David Chipperfield Architects.

8: Belgo Bar & Restaurant, London.
Ph: C. Kicherer

9: Belgo Bar & Restaurant, London.
Ph: C. Kicherer

10: "Tinker Chair", 1988.
Mild steel and stainless steel handmade chair with stainless steel welds. Each chair is forced into shape by panel-beating.
Ph: Howard Kingsnorth

11: "38 Tables", 1995.
38 tables of varying shape and size, each one produced in a limited edition of 38. The structure is based on a spine with regularly spaced cantilevers. Mirror polished stainless steel and patinated steel.

12: "Fly on the Wall", 1994.
A cube in eight sections connected to each other via hinges. The cube can disintegrate to provide a variety of different shelving shapes. As the cube requires wall fixing at only two points the form of the shelf can vary at will after installation.

13: The New Tel Aviv Opera
Architects: Ron Arad/ Alison Brooks
Foyer building showing box office.
Ph: G. Dagon

14: Adidas Stadium, Paris
Computer image showing travelator.

15: The New Tel Aviv Opera
Amphitheatre stairs in bronze leading to Mezzanine level.
Architects: Ron Arad/ Alison Brooks
Ph: C. Kicherer

16: Chalk Farm Studios, London
General view of own studio.
Architect: Ron Arad

17: "Looploop", 1992
A continuous loop of flexible woven stainless steel welded into high backed, flexible black steel chair profiles, leaving a loop at top and bottom.
Design: Ron Arad
Ph: Christoph Kicherer

18: "Bookworm", 1993.
Wall mounted book shelves in blackened strip tempered steel. The form is retained by "fake books" or box brackets - size is unlimited and the form varies with each installation.
Design Ron Arad
Ph: Christoph Kicherer

19: Fondation Cartier, Paris, 1994.
An installation to accommodate performing arts events, both performers and audience. 30 mirrors polished stainless steel tables arranged on the floor in a paving pattern, like tiles. Both the tables and the gaps between them can be used by both public and performers.
Artist: Ron Arad
Installation fabricated by Marzorati Ronchetti, Italy
Ph: Peter Willi

20: "Shadow of Time"
Decorated or chromed steel hollow cone shaped light. Clock movement casts a shadow of the time on wall or ceiling. Adjustable angle. 500w halogen bulb. Dimmer.
Ph: S. Muto

21: "Three Thirds of a Table", 1989
Vaguely circular table in three integral parts. The top surface becomes the legs. The legs were originally made three inches longer and have been shortened by beating and hammering.

Also available from Dis Voir

ÉDITIONS DIS VOIR : 3, RUE BEAUTREILLIS - F-75004 PARIS
PHONE (33 - 1) 48 87 07 09 - FAX (33 - 1) 48 87 07 14